**Melanie**
To Caitlin, my twin flame and little latke,
and to the Jewish-Latinx community that
welcomed us home.

**Cassie**
To Mama, who chose my books,
and to Daddy, who read them to me.

 LIBROS

www.LilLibros.com

J is for Janucá
Published by Little Libros, LLC

Text © 2022 Little Libros, LLC
Art © 2022 Casandra Gonzales
Designed by Haydeé Yañez

Library of Congress Control Number 2021953208

Printed in China
First Edition – 2022
27 26 25 24 23 22   5 4 3 2 1

ISBN 978-1-948066-42-6

# J is for

# JANUCÁ

BY MELANIE ROMERO

Illustrated by CASSIE GONZALES

# Aa is for Aceite / Oil

The Jews used a small amount of olive oil to light the Holy Temple's menorah that miraculously burned for eight days straight when it was believed that the oil would only last for one day.

Los judíos utilizaron una pequeña cantidad de aceite de oliva para encender la menorá del Templo Sagrado que, milagrosamente, ardió durante ocho días seguidos cuando se creía que el aceite sólo duraría un día.

# Bb is for Bendiciones

## Blessings

There are many blessings recited during this holiday, especially when lighting the candles.

Hay muchas bendiciones que se recitan durante esta fiesta, especialmente al encender las velas.

# Cc is for Celebración
## Celebration

Hanukkah is a special holiday meant to be celebrated with family and friends.

Januká es una fiesta especial que se celebra con la familia y los amigos.

# CHch is for Chocolate

Chocolate

Hanukkah gelt (which means "money" in Yiddish) refers to presents given to children during the holiday, typically in the form of gold-foiled chocolate coins.

El gelt de Janucá (que significa "dinero" en yidis) se refiere a los regalos que se dan a los niños durante la fiesta, normalmente en forma de monedas de chocolate forradas con papel dorado.

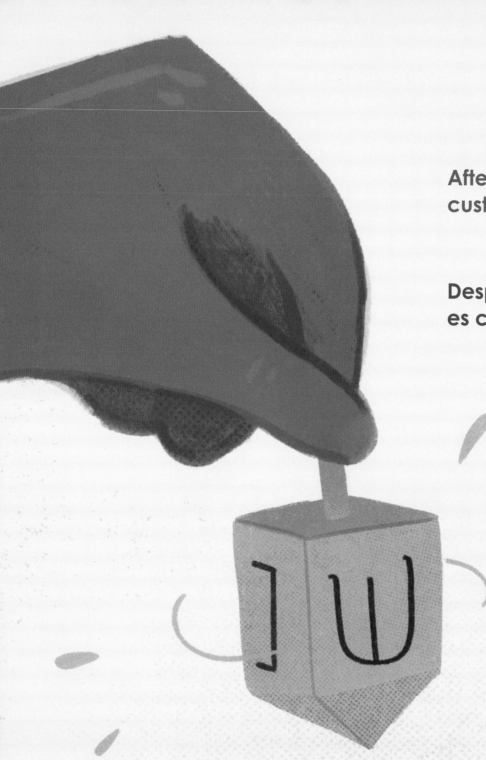

After lighting the candles, it is customary to play dreidel.

Después de encender las velas, es costumbre jugar dreidel.

**Dd** is for Dreidel

Dreidel

# Ee is for Estrella de David / Star of David

The Star of David is a worldwide recognized symbol of modern Jewish identity.

La Estrella de David es un símbolo mundialmente reconocido de la identidad judía moderna.

# Ff is for Frito

## Fried

Frito stands for the fried foods that Jewish families prepare and eat throughout the holiday to celebrate the miracle of the oil.

Frito representa los alimentos fritos que las familias judías preparan y comen durante toda la fiesta para celebrar el milagro del aceite.

# Gg is for _Gimel_
## _Gimel_

"Gimel" is the phonetic word for the English letter, "g," of the dreidel. If someone lands on gimel, they get to take the jackpot!

"Guímel" es la palabra fonética de la letra inglesa "g" del dreidel. Si caen en guímel, ¡se llevan el premio mayor!

# Hh is for <u>Hogar</u>
## Home

One makes a home with their family and friends once the celebration begins. *Mazel tov!*

Una vez que comience la celebración, uno hace un hogar con su familia y sus amigos. *¡Mazel tov!*

# Ii is for Iluminación
## Illumination

Hanukkah candles cast the most beautiful light! One lights the candles starting from the left and working to the right.

¡Las velas de Janucá proyectan la luz más hermosa! Uno enciende las velas empezando de la izquierda hacia la derecha.

# Jj is for Januça / Hanukkah

Another name for Hanukkah is the Festival of Lights. This holiday honors the revolution of the Maccabees and the miracle of oil hundreds of years ago.

Otro nombre para Januçá es el Festival de las Luces. Esta fiesta honra la revolución de los macabeos y el milagro del aceite hace cientos de años.

# Kk is for Kugel / Kugel

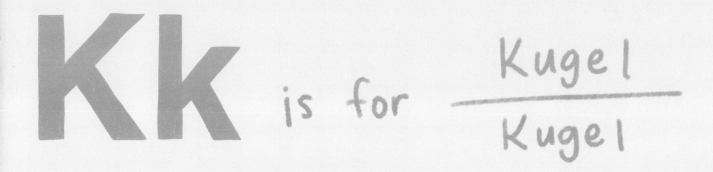

Kugel is a baked casserole commonly made from egg noodles or potatoes. It can be sweet or savory! Although kugel is German for "globe," it is actually baked in square pans.

El kugel es una cazuela al horno que suele hacerse con fideos de huevo o papas. ¡Puede ser dulce o salado! Aunque en alemán kugel significa "globo," en realidad se hornea en cacerolas cuadradas.

# Ll is for Latke
## Latke

Latke is a word in Hebrew that comes from Russian, translating to "little pancake." It is a fried potato pancake that is traditionally accompanied by applesauce and sour cream as dips. The crispier, the better!

Latke es una palabra hebrea que proviene del ruso y que se traduce como "pequeña tortita." Es una tortita de papa frita que tradicionalmente se acompaña con puré de manzana y crema agria. Cuanto más crujiente sea el latke, ¡mejor!

# Ll is for Lleno / Full

A home is full of love (and homemade food) during this time of year.

En esta época del año estamos llenos de amor
(y de comida casera).

# Mm is for Menorá / Menorah

A menorah is a candelabra with eight main branches, plus the raised ninth lamp set apart as the *shamash* used to kindle the other lights.

Una menorá es un candelabro con ocho ramas principales, más la novena lámpara elevada que se aparta como luz del *shamash* que se utiliza para encender las otras velas.

# Nn is for Noche
## Night

Hanukkah is celebrated over the course of eight days because of the miraculous oil that lasted for eight days. Each night at sundown, family and friends gather to light a candle for that day.

Janucá se celebra durante ocho días debido al aceite milagroso que duró ocho días. Cada noche, al ocaso, la familia y los amigos se reúnen para encender la vela de ese día.

# Ññ is for Año / year

★ KISLEV

| | | 1 | 2 | 3 | 4 | 5 |
|---|---|---|---|---|---|---|
| 6 | 7 | 8 | 9 | 10 | 11 | 12 |
| 13 | 14 | 15 | 16 | 17 | 18 | 19 |
| 20 | 21 | 22 | 23 | 24 | 25 First Night! | 26 |
| 27 | 28 | 29 | 30 | | | |

The Hebrew calendar follows the moon. The moon phases direct us on when to celebrate important dates of the Jewish year, like Hanukkah.

El calendario hebreo sigue a la luna. Las fases lunares nos indican cuándo celebrar fechas importantes del año judío, como la Janucá.

# Oo is for ___Ocaso___ / ___Sunset___

At sunset, families gather around the menorah to light the candles.

Al ocaso, las familias se juntan alrededor de la menorá para encender las velas.

8 7 6 5     4 3 2 1

# Pp is for Papas
## Potatoes

During Hanukah, potatoes are beloved. For holiday dinners, potatoes are grated into patties and shallow-fried into latkes.

Durante Janucá, las papas son muy amadas. Durante las cenas festivas, las papas se rallan en tortitas y se fríen a poca profundidad para hacer latkes.

# Qq is for ___Queridos___
## Loved Ones

Together, beloved friends and family members make Hanukkah so special.

Juntos, queridos amigos y familiares hacen que Janucá sea muy especial.

# Rr is for Regalos / Gifts

Like other holidays during this season, one gives gifts during Hanukkah. However, gift-giving has become an American-Jewish phenomenon because gift-giving is not traditionally part of Hanukkah at all.

Al igual que en otras fiestas de esta época, en Janucá se dan regalos. Sin embargo, la entrega de regalos se ha convertido en un fenómeno judío-estadounidense, ya que tradicionalmente la entrega de regalos no forma parte de Janucá.

# RRrr is for _Tierra_
## Land

Families gather during this holiday to remember the land that their Jewish ancestors left behind.

Las familias se reúnen durante esta fiesta para recordar la tierra que dejaron sus antepasados judíos.

# Ss is for Sufganiyot

Sufganiyot

Sufganiyot are deep-fried doughnuts eaten during the celebration of Hanukkah. The doughnut is deep-fried in oil, filled with jam, custard, or chocolate, and then topped with powdered sugar. Delicious!

Las *sufganiyot* son donas fritas que se comen durante la celebración de Janucá. La dona se fríe en aceite, se rellena con mermelada, crema o chocolate y se cubre con azúcar en polvo. ¡Son deliciosas!

# Tt is for Templo / Temple

Temple, also called a synagogue or shul in Yiddish, is the place of worship for the Jewish people, and they honor their beliefs in its very walls and beyond.

Templo, también conocido como sinagoga o shul en yidis, es el lugar de culto de los judíos, y ellos honran sus creencias en sus paredes mismas y más allá.

# Uu is for <u>Unidos</u> <u>united</u>

Communities have continued to unite in celebrating Hanukkah and all its traditions for so many generations and the more to come.

Las comunidades han continuado unidas celebrando Janucá y todas sus tradiciones durante muchas generaciones y las que están por venir.

# Vv is for _Velas_
## Candles

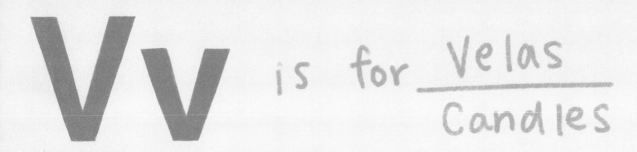

One must remember to gather the Hanukkah candles before the festivities: they are the tools we light in celebration.

Hay que acordarse de recolectar las velas de Janucá antes de las festividades: son las herramientas que encendemos para celebrar.

# Ww is for Wisdom
## Sabiduría

Jewish wisdom and spirituality is as old as the Torah itself. The Hamsa, a highly respected hand-shaped symbol, holds its power on Kabbalistic amulets and spiritual objects.

La sabiduría y la espiritualidad judías son tan antiguas como la propia Torá. El Hamsa, un símbolo muy respetado en forma de mano, mantiene su poder en amuletos cabalísticos y objetos espirituales.

# Xx is for Exilio / Exile

During Hanukkah, families remember the Jewish exile, or the forced migration of Jews from their homeland to other parts of the world.

Durante Janucá, las familias recuerdan el exilio judío, o la migración forzada de los judíos desde su patria a otras partes del mundo.

# Yy is for _Yidis_

Yiddish

Yiddish is a German-derived language historically spoken by Jewish people in central and eastern Europe. It is a dialect from German with words from Hebrew and other modern languages.

El yidis es una lengua derivada del alemán, hablada históricamente por el pueblo judío en Europa central y del Este. Es un dialecto del alemán con palabras del hebreo y otras lenguas modernas.

# Zz is for _Zzzz_ / _Zzzz_

Zzzz. Thank you for reading and good night – until next Hanukkah!

Zzzz. Gracias por leer y buenas noches – ¡hasta la próxima Janucá!

# THE STORY OF HANUKKAH

More than 2,000 years ago, the Jewish people lived in peace in Judea. However, Antiochus – a Greek ruler – soon took power in Judea and ordered the Jewish people to follow beliefs unlike their own. Antiochus banned all Jewish rituals; the Jewish people could no longer observe Shabbat (Judaism's day of rest: Saturday) or any other custom. Antiochus defiled the Temple by installing an altar to Zeus Olympios and ordered the Jewish people to pray to Greek gods. A small band of Jews, known as the Maccabees, rebelled against Antiochus; Mattathias and his son, Judah, headed the rebellion. After a long war, the Maccabees defeated Antiochus and drove away his soldiers. The Jewish people regained control of their land, but their Temple was left in ruins. They cleaned and repaired the Temple. To celebrate their victory and to rededicate the Temple, they relit the ner tamid of the menorah, an "eternal flame" that was always to be burning in the Temple, which is still symbolized above the ark in temples today, with a small cruse of oil. It was only enough to last a day. The messenger who was sent to secure additional oil took eight days to complete his mission and believed the Temple would be without oil when he returned. But, the small supply of oil continued to burn until the eighth day. **A miracle.** That is why the eight days of Hanukkah can be attributed to the miracle of this single jar of oil.

# LA HISTORIA DE JANUCÁ

Hace más de 2.000 años, el pueblo judío vivía en paz en Judea. Sin embargo, Antíoco – un gobernante griego – pronto tomó el poder en Judea y ordenó al pueblo judío que siguiera creencias distintas a las suyas. Antíoco prohibió todos los rituales judíos; el pueblo judío ya no podía observar el sabbat (el día de descanso del judaísmo: el sábado) ni ninguna otra costumbre. Antíoco profanó el Templo instalando un altar a Zeus Olímpico y ordenó al pueblo judío que rezara a los dioses griegos. Un pequeño grupo de judíos, conocido como los macabeos, se rebeló contra Antíoco; Matatías y su hijo, Judá, encabezaron la rebelión. Tras una larga guerra, los macabeos derrotaron a Antíoco y expulsaron a sus soldados. El pueblo judío recuperó el control de su tierra, pero su Templo quedó en ruinas. Limpiaron y repararon el Templo. Para celebrar su victoria y volver a consagrar el Templo, volvieron a encender el ner tamid de la menorá, una "llama eterna" que debía estar siempre encendida en el Templo, y que aún hoy se simboliza sobre el arca en los templos, con una pequeña vasija de aceite. Sólo era suficiente para un día. El mensajero que fue enviado a conseguir aceite adicional tardó ocho días en completar su misión y creyó que el Templo estaría sin aceite cuando regresara. Pero, el pequeño suministro de aceite continuó ardiendo hasta el octavo día. Un milagro. Por eso, los ocho días de Janucá pueden atribuirse al milagro de esta única jarra de aceite.